This book is dedicated to all who cherish America's history as a vast heritage of people and events—some heroic, some inglorious, but all part of America's epic struggle to come of age—and to all who know that understanding the past is essential to dealing with the present.

D0608254

ANDERSONVILLE
THE STORY BEHIND THE SCENERY®
by Michael Alan Marsh

Alan Marsh has been employed by the National Park Service since 1985, most recently as Cultural Resources Specialist for both Andersonville and Jimmy Carter National Historic Sites. Alan, a published author, received his master's degree in history from Georgia College.

Photography by Robert Creamer, who specializes in large format photography. His clients include architects, interior designers, museums, and the National Park Service. Bob presents fine-art landscape photography workshops at Yosemite, Arches, and Yellowstone.

Andersonville National Historic Site, *in southwest Georgia, was established in 1970 to commemorate the sacrifices of Americans who lost their lives in prisoner of war camps.*

Front cover: Stockade wall and Providence Spring; Inside front cover: Massachusetts and Ohio monuments; photos by Bob Creamer. Page 1: Memorial Day tribute from a grateful nation; photo by Alan Marsh. Pages 2 and 3: New Jersey Monument above a sea of marble; photo by Bob Creamer.

Edited by Cheri C. Madison. Book design by K. C. DenDooven.

"If need be I would die for the flag
and what it stands for—
but that's what freedom is."

—JESSE MOORE, World War II Prisoner of War

Andersonville Prison Camp

In January 1864, the tall pine forest just east of Andersonville, Georgia, began to fall under the swing of axes. The residents of the small southwest Georgia town watched with apprehension and anticipation as slaves from local farms raised the hewn logs upright and the 15-foot-high walls fell into place. Camp Sumter, a prisoner of war camp for Union soldiers, would receive its first inhabitants in mid-February. The tranquillity of the peaceful Georgia town would soon vanish. In its place would be such pain and suffering that for years to come, indeed centuries, just the mention of the name Andersonville would evoke images of man's inhumanity to man.

At the outbreak of the American Civil War, few imagined that it would drag on for four long years. Neither northern nor southern armies were adequately prepared for war, much less for prisoners of war. Initially, prisoners captured on the battlefield were exchanged by the commanding officers after the battle, but soon a formal exchange system was accepted by both governments. The system eventually collapsed due to disagreements between the two sides. There were charges of unfair exchange practices and controversy over the use of Black soldiers—plus the North realized that the Confederacy benefited the most from the exchange system. The North had manpower reserves that could not be matched by the South and, if exchanges were ceased, Confederate soldiers could no longer quickly return to the ranks. Soon after the collapse, prison facilities in both North and South became severely overcrowded.

The Confederacy housed many of its captives in and around Richmond, Virginia. Fearing that the proximity of these prisoners to the front lines of war created a hazard, the government began a search for a more suitable location. The search led Captain W. Sidney Winder to Georgia and, eventually, to Andersonville.

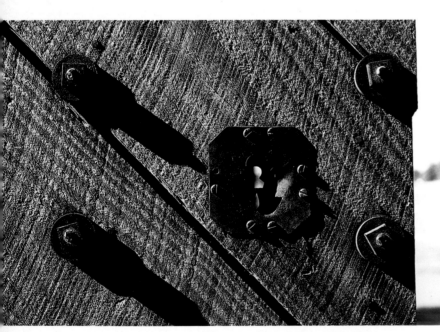

"Arrived at our destination at last and a dismal hole it is too," wrote prisoner of war John Ransom of the 7th Michigan Cavalry. Every Union soldier stood outside the North Gate, listened as key met lock, and watched as their portal to hell opened.

Guard towers, known as "pigeon roosts," stand silently above the reconstructed stockade wall. The pine logs serve as reminders of those who gave part or all of their lives to Andersonville—the slaves who built it, the boys and men who stood guard in its towers, and the prisoners who languished within. For 14 months, walls such as these kept the inhabitants separated from the outside world, far away from home and family.

LOCATION OF THE NEW CAMP

Captain Winder examined two sites in Georgia—Radium Springs near Albany, and Magnolia Springs located between Americus and Plains. Local opposition to these locations led Winder to look elsewhere. Finally, he was directed to Andersonville, a small town on the Southwestern Railroad, ten miles north of Americus. Two land owners, Benjamin Dykes and Wesley Turner, were willing to rent land at what seemed to be an ideal site. The area was covered in pine trees which could be cut to form stockade walls, the surrounding area was agricultural, and a small stream divided two hillsides. Perhaps most importantly, it was conveniently located only a couple hundred yards from the Southwestern Railroad and the Andersonville depot. A deal was made and construction began on a 16 1/2-acre wooden stockade to house 6,000 enlisted Union prisoners of war.

The stockade walls were not finished when the first Union prisoners of war arrived at the Andersonville depot in mid February 1864 and were marched towards the prison pen. Once through the massive wooden North Gate, they got their first full view of the interior—two hillsides, dropping abruptly to a sluggish stream below. Although it was not the most appealing environment, these new arrivals found conditions at Camp Sumter more favorable than their previous home at Belle Isle, a mosquito-infested island in the James River at Richmond.

The 16 1/2-acre Andersonville stockade provided ample room, although there were no barracks for housing. Tree branches that littered the ground were collected by the new arrivals for firewood and to construct makeshift shelters or "shebangs." The stream, named Stockade Branch, provided an adequate water supply. These conditions would soon deteriorate as the

As the camp's population increased, prisoners were used to enlarge the northern end of the stockade by ten acres. From the northeast corner of the stockade, Confederate guards looked out from their sentry posts upon shelter halves, gum blankets, wooden lean-tos, and other temporary shelters constructed by those interned below. Occasionally, locals ventured into the guard towers to view their unwilling guests. The deadline and wall were all that separated prisoners from guards and it could not contain the smell of human filth that hung heavily over the prison camp and neighboring town.

Today the serenity of the prison camp belies the horror and suffering of those unfortunate enough to have found themselves confined here during the last 14 months of the Civil War. Forests covered the entire ground prior to construction of the prison camp. Over time, trees have once again claimed much of the area, broken only by earthen fortifications, the grassy plain of the stockade, and brown vegetation which was once the site of the hospital. The obelisk of the Ohio Monument points skyward from the prison grounds. The National Prisoner of War Museum rises out from the tree line, just beyond the stockade walls of the northeast corner.

number of prisoners increased and the Confederacy became even more strapped for resources.

By May, conditions had already started to wane. The guard force, composed of the 55th, 56th, and 57th Georgia Infantry, along with the 26th Alabama Infantry, was replaced by regiments of the Georgia Reserves. The reserves, composed of young boys and old men, had little military training or experience. In addition, the prison population continued to increase. By June, the number of internees had risen to 25,000.

DAILY SURVIVAL

As summer approached, conditions at Andersonville worsened. The prisoners no longer faced an enemy on the battlefield, but every day was a fight for survival. Food, water, and shelter were at a premium. The Union soldiers sought ways to break the monotony of each hot summer day. A variety of games were played, including cards, checkers, chess, and dominoes. One popular game was "grayback" racing.

Named for the gray uniform of the guards, "graybacks" was the name the prisoners of war gave to the abundant lice. Lice were placed in the center of heated tin pans and men shouted encouragement to their favorite, urging it towards the finish line of the pan edge. More than just a passive means of biding time, the competition often involved wagers of food or items of value. A little skill or good luck might keep one alive another day. A loss could add to one's misery.

Food was also available within the prison camp—but there was a price to be paid. A wooden structure, initially a short distance inside the stockade from the North Gate, provided space for a sutler to operate. A variety of food could be obtained at the store. During late June and early July in 1864, the price of one egg was 50 cents, a pint of black beans, 40 cents. Many prisoners found that trading and stealing were more economical means of obtaining nourishment.

The overcrowded, haphazard arrangement of "shebangs" and the daily existence of the forlorn prisoners were captured by photographer A. J. Riddle in August 1864. By Christmas, the heat of summer had given way to winter when George W. Pennington, 57th Pennsylvania Infantry, wrote "weather cold and disagreeable. We sit around our scanty fires shivering and hungry, thinking what good times we might enjoy were we permitted to be at home."

The thoughts and dreams of food grew incessantly stronger, especially by late summer when a day's ration consisted of a handful of cornmeal. Diaries echoed the thoughts of food. "Hannah, I often dream of you and ham and eggs but don't get a chance to eat with you," wrote William Peabody of the 57th Massachusetts Infantry on July 31, 1864. He never received the chance. One month later, on September 2, William Peabody died.

Six and a half months after the camp opened, Private William T. Peabody, 57th Massachusetts Infantry, succumbed to diarrhea. He became the 7,556th victim of Andersonville. Now, generations later, Peabody and other prisoners at Andersonville are more than numbers; they are the epitome of sacrifice, courage, and dedication to country.

Bedraggled and unkempt in appearance, prisoners and their crude shelters greet the arrival of the ration wagon at the North Gate on a hot August day in 1864. In the background, the sutler shanty rises above the crowd. Prisoners also established businesses, and several located along "Market Street" provided the sutler with keen competition. Despite the crowds and activities within the prison, loneliness was a constant companion of many prisoners. Levi Whitaker, a private with the 11th Connecticut Infantry, confided to his journal that "this morning is fine weather but there is very many sad and heavy hearts in this pen it is a gloom place to spend the 4th of July.... I am in the Bull pen sad and lonely tonight."

Looking west across the width of the prison, the eye gazes upon one of the gently sloping hills that rise above the camp's water supply. The channel is narrower today, but the waters of Stockade Branch still flow sluggishly through the prison camp. The water gives birth to lush vegetation where dirt and mud were once trod by soldiers making their way to drink, bathe, and use the latrine.

PRISON WATER

Water was also essential to life. Prisoners were allowed to dig wells, and a few were successful. Those who succeeded found that a lucrative business could be made by selling their commodity to those less fortunate. The primary water supply was the small stream that flowed through the camp, but Stockade Branch quickly became a quagmire of pollution and filth. The water was used by both the guard force and the bakehouse before it entered the prison. As it made its way through the cracks of the prison's timber walls, it became the source of drinking water for the prisoners. As it continued through the camp, it was utilized for bathing and washing of clothes.

The lower end, just before it exited the stockade, was where the sinks, or latrines, were built. Many of the soldiers were in ill health, and diarrhea and dysentery were rampant in camp. The two hillsides above the stream were covered with the filth of those unable, or unwilling, to make the trek down to the sinks. Frequent rains washed the filth downhill and into the stream below, leaving a colored film of waste throughout the prison valley after each shower ended and the water dissipated.

By August 1864, life was almost unbearable at the Andersonville prison. Skeletons of humani-

ty slowly stirred within the log walls, desperately clinging to thoughts of freedom and home. Rations consisted of a handful of cornmeal, living space was limited to a six foot by four foot area, and the death rate exceeded 100 persons each day. Ironically, during this horrific month, an event occurred which provided a source of hope and thanksgiving for many of the forlorn prisoners of war.

Heavy rainfall created a flood through the low area surrounding the stream. As the water receded, a spring appeared, providing a much needed water supply. The new source, however, was located within the "deadline," an area 19 feet within the stockade wall and marked by a 4-foot-high rail. The rail formed a perimeter around the entire camp and was designed to keep prisoners away from the wall and under the watchful eyes of the guards. Prisoners were well aware that the

Many prisoner diaries record with thanksgiving the story of a wonderful spring that gushed forth from the ground during an August storm in 1864. Some say it was caused by lightning; others insist that the heavy rains uncovered it. The cause may be argued but the cool waters of Providence Spring still flow from the earth, surrounded by a granite and marble memorial constructed in 1901.

Engrained in the consciousness of Union veterans, and engraved in the stone of the Iowa Monument, the story of Providence Spring illustrates the importance of faith to prisoners of war.

guards would fulfill their orders and shoot anyone crossing the line. Captain Wirz, the Confederate officer in charge of the stockade interior, allowed the men to construct a flume to channel the water inside the prison. The spring, attributed as an answer to prayer, was named Providence Spring.

In contrast to the open prison camp, the shade of hardwood trees and the calm waters of the Providence Spring reflecting pool provide a few moments of respite and tranquillity. It is a perfect place to contemplate the past and reflect on the horrors and deprivations of Andersonville.

Two sides, divided not only by loyalty to a cause but by a line of timbers. Each longed for family and home, each anticipated the end of war. "If it weren't for hope the heart would break. And I am hopeful yet," wrote one prisoner of war.

As the prison population increased, the supply of wood within the prison camp quickly decreased. In addition to wood-gathering details, burial details were a means of acquiring the sought-after commodity, which was used to build shelters, cook rations, and provide warmth. Like other commodities, wood could be obtained from fellow prisoners—for a price.

Sixteen artillery pieces, Napoleons and three-inch ordnance rifles, overlooked the prison and discouraged mass uprisings or escape attempts. Most of the artillery that guarded the camp were Federal guns captured at Olustee, Florida, one week before Andersonville opened.

Irregular lines of earth mark the perimeter of the Star Fort, the command center of Andersonville Prison. In addition to guards and artillery, the fortification contained a powder magazine and the headquarters of Captain Henry Wirz, the Confederate officer in charge of the prisoners. The fort occupied the highest ground and was an ideal observation post for the camp.

In the years following the war, seeds found root in the loose soil of wells and tunnels dug by desperate men. Tunneling was a favorite pastime and created a great deal of concern among camp administrators. The soil of the camp, a combination of clay and sand, was not conducive to digging— but that did not deter many from trying their best with hands, sticks, and broken canteens. The lack of wood to support the tunnel, the likelihood of a fellow prisoner turning you in for extra rations, and the threat of having to spend a week locked in stocks were additional obstacles. As a result, most of the successful escapes came from fleeing work details, not through tunnels.

13

The South Gate was one of two located along the western line of the stockade wall. Each morning a wagon rolled in with the day's rations, and each afternoon the same wagon arrived to take out the dead. The medical staff also entered daily to record illnesses and take requests for medicine and treatment. For many prisoners who exited the gate bound for the hospital, it would be their last day at the prison.

MEDICAL CONDITIONS

As might be expected, diseases flourished at the prison camp. Medical reports and death records show that diarrhea, dysentery, scurvy, and pneumonia took their toll. Smallpox also broke out among the prisoners. Confederate medical personnel moved smallpox patients to a location two miles south of town and began inoculations of prisoners. The inoculations commonly turned gangrenous, causing rumors to circulate among the Union soldiers that it was a deliberate attempt to kill them.

The Confederate medical personnel at Andersonville faced a daunting challenge. Every morning at 7:00 a.m., prisoners requesting medical treatment or admission to the hospital proceeded to the South Gate. One hour later, Confederate medical personnel arrived at 12 booths set up near the gate. The line of prisoners began to move slowly forward as doctors and paroled prisoners took names and recorded the nature of each illness. In July and August of 1864, the average number of Union soldiers who congregated at the booths each day numbered between 3,000 and 4,000.

Medicine was hard to acquire. Requisitions had to be sent to Atlanta for approval and often could not be filled. The Confederate government had a war to fight, and a prisoner of war camp in southwest Georgia was not its primary concern.

Medical supplies were not the only items that camp staff had trouble acquiring. Tents, blankets, and clothing were also in short supply. A common method of obtaining additional clothing was to strip the dead prior to burial.

Once the dead were taken from the stockade or hospital, they were placed in the "dead house," a makeshift structure where they were kept until the half-mile journey to the cemetery. On August 16, 1864, this detail of Union soldiers paused from its solemn task for a photograph.

COURTESY OF ANDERSONVILLE NATIONAL HISTORIC SITE

THE RAIDERS AND THE REGULATORS

The lack of proper sanitation and basic items needed for survival, such as food and water, made life at the Andersonville prison a horrible existence. Unfortunately, matters were made worse by an element of the prison population known as the "Raiders." These gangs, which numbered a couple of hundred in some reports, were ruthless bands that stole food, clothing, and valuables from their peers. As their numbers grew, so did their boldness. Beating and stealing eventually led to outright murder of fellow prisoners.

Finally, other prisoners made a stand against these vicious gangs. Led by "Limber Jim," a police force known as the Regulators was formed. Many of the Raiders were rounded up and turned over to camp authorities for punishment. A trial was held for the six gang leaders. The jury, 24 Union sergeants who had recently arrived, listened to the defense and prosecution. After deliberation, the verdict was returned: guilty. The six would be hung. Gallows were constructed and on July 11, 1864, Captain Wirz allowed the prisoners to carry out the sentence.

Life was also difficult for the Confederate guards at Andersonville. The first through fourth regiments of the Georgia Reserves comprised the guard force for most of the camp's existence, including late summer when conditions were the worst.

Basked in sunlight but not in glory lie the graves of the Raiders. They claimed they were good people, driven to do bad things by conditions at Andersonville. Their alibi was not believed, and the leaders were hanged for murder.

The boys and old men of the Reserves suffered from the same diseases and inadequate provisions as the prisoners. A report made in August 1864 listed over 1,200 guards either sick, on leave, or absent without leave. By the end of the war, 249 had died.

THE END?

As summer gave way to fall in 1864, Confederate authorities at Andersonville became increasingly worried. General Sherman was making his way through Georgia, and many feared that he would attempt to liberate the prisoners of war at Camp Sumter. To prevent this, the Confederacy began to relocate prisoners from Andersonville to other sites such as Camp Lawton in Millen, Georgia, and Camp Florence in South Carolina. A contingent of Sherman's army, led by General Stoneman, did plan to liberate Union officers imprisoned in Macon and enlisted personnel at Andersonville. The attempt was stymied outside of Macon. Many of Stoneman's men did travel the 65 miles from Macon to Andersonville—as prisoners of war instead of liberators.

Most of the soldiers relocated to other prison camps returned to Andersonville after the threat from Sherman was over. On December 25, 1864, two groups of 500 weary prisoners of war returned to the stockade. The last contingent arrived the next day. There was not much cause for celebration as their new year approached. Indeed, as

The emotional and physical toil of being a prisoner of war is etched eternally in bronze on the New York Monument.

the Confederacy continued to crumble and Union forces continued to move through the South, many Andersonville prisoners felt forsaken. Although exchanges were resumed in January 1865, soldiers continued to languish in Camp Sumter. Union troops did not arrive at the prison camp until May, weeks after the war's end.

An American eagle proudly perches atop the Wisconsin Monument. Words inscribed into the monument in honor of Union dead still hold special meaning to former prisoners of war who visit and volunteer at Andersonville: "To live in hearts we leave behind is not to die."

"As the heavy wooden door closed behind us my heart sank within me and such a sense of utter and hopeless desolation crept over me as I hope never to feel again," wrote G. E. Reynolds. Andersonville prisoners passed through two sets of wooden double doors to enter the camp. The outside doors led into a small holding area, and the second set opened to the interior of the stockade. Soldiers on the inside would gather en masse to greet new arrivals ("fresh fish") and receive news of the war and outside world.

The memory of Andersonville was etched into the mind of every soldier who survived the experience. Between 1879 and 1885 Thomas O'Dea, formerly of the 16th Maine Infantry, devoted his leisure time to producing a superb illustration of Andersonville Prison.

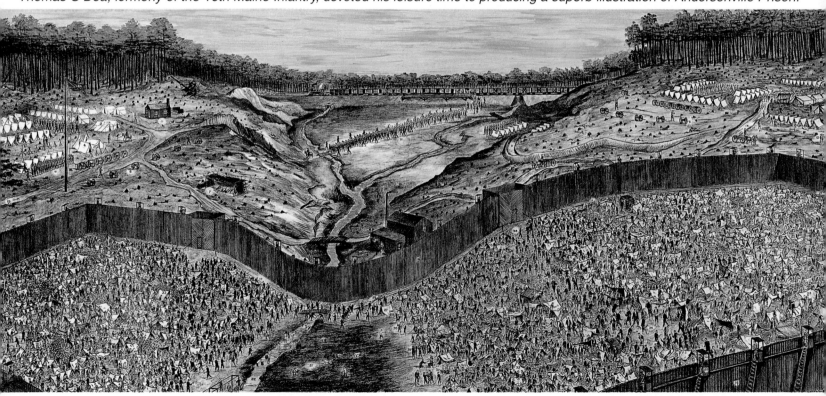

Andersonville National Cemetery

At sunrise on August 17, 1865, the United States flag slowly ascended the wooden pole, reached the top, and unfurled in the gentle August wind. Clara Barton stood at the base of the flagpole and looked up at the stars and stripes she had just raised. After "The Star-Spangled Banner," three volleys were fired and the ceremony was over. That night, the Civil War nurse wrote in her diary, "the work was done: my own hands have helped to run up the old flag on our great and holy ground and I ought to be satisfied. I believe I am."

For many of the 45,000 Union prisoners at Andersonville, death had been the only escape.

Adam Swarner, the first casualty of Andersonville. Five months later, his brother Jacob was buried in grave number 4,005.

Overcrowding and the lack of proper food, water, and shelter all contributed to the physical and mental demise of many Union soldiers. During the 14 months of the camp's existence 12,914 perished. They were buried side by side, shoulder to shoulder, in shallow graves. Numbered wooden posts were placed at the graves, and entries made in the burial register recorded the grave number, name, regiment, and date of death of the deceased. For 460 soldiers, only the word "Unknown" was written in the register.

Marble stones reach up to meet the rays of the morning sun. As the warm glow bathes the cemetery, a granite figure silently weeps for the sons of Iowa who lie below. The state of Iowa approved $10,000 for the monument and appointed five former prisoners of war to the commission charged with erecting a suitable monument "commemorative of the valor, suffering and martyrdom of the Iowa soldiers." Time has done much to heal the wounds of war, but the sacrifice of all the soldiers entombed in the serene landscape will never be forgotten.

The Clara Barton Monument, erected in honor of the founder of the American Red Cross.

In each quadrant of the national cemetery, huge magnolias stretch forth their limbs from beneath broad leaf canopies. After the Civil War, Clara Barton turned her attention from nursing the sick and wounded to identifying the location of Union dead. Her endeavors brought her to Andersonville during the summer of 1865 where she helped identify graves, dedicated the cemetery, and planted flowering trees, very likely the magnolias.

Dorence Atwater of the 2nd New York Cavalry was a teenager when he arrived at Andersonville as a prisoner of war. As a hospital clerk, he kept a list of the dead. After the war, Atwater insisted the list be published but could not persuade the U.S. government to agree. A dispute ensued—and Atwater was arrested for theft, court martialed, and sent to a New York penitentiary. Soon the court martial was overturned, Atwater released, and the list published.

Thanks to the efforts of Confederate staff and paroled prisoners such as Atwater, only 460 Union soldiers were buried as unknown.

Accompanying Miss Barton to Andersonville were Captain James Moore, 34 laborers, and Dorence Atwater. During his internment at the Andersonville prison, Atwater had been responsible for recording entries into the burial register. He had made a duplicate copy of the list and smuggled this copy out of camp when he left in February of 1865. Using Atwater's list and captured rolls, the party began their work of identifying the graves. Wooden headboards were cut, and the names of deceased prisoners of war painted on them. These replaced the numbered posts marking each grave. The work was finally complete, and on August 17 the dedication ceremony was held and the flag raised over the national cemetery. Beneath its stars and stripes lay the final resting place of almost 13,000 Union soldiers.

ALL KINDS OF HEROES

Andersonville is proof that patriotism and devotion to duty are not owned by any particular race, age, or sex. Among the dead at Andersonville are African Americans, American Indians, Caucasians, and Hispanics. Interred in the hallowed ground are young boys and civilians, as well as immigrants who left their homeland in search of a better way of life in America.

There were also women at Andersonville. Reportedly, several women were quartered outside the stockade. Two were able to conceal their identities and live inside the walls of the Andersonville prison, among the other prisoners of war. The identity of one, Florena Budwin, was discovered after her transfer to Camp Florence Prison. The identity of the other may always remain a mystery. Only upon her death was her secret discovered. The words "Unknown Lady Soldier" were recorded in the burial register.

Prisoners of war at Andersonville, like other camps North and South, could have received their freedom from confinement with the mere stroke of a pen. A signed oath of allegiance to the Confederacy, a promise to fight for a former enemy, and release would have been granted. Instead, almost 13,000 chose death rather than to dishonor themselves, their families, and their country.

In evening's light, eternal memorials stand watch over the Andersonville dead. A young soldier, disarmed, gazes across the hallowed grounds from his granite pedestal. Connecticut chose the simple yet strong bronze figure to honor its sons who were interned at the prison camp. In the distance is the Iowa Monument.

Not only Andersonville prisoners of war are honored in the national cemetery. Americans held as prisoners of war in Stalag XVII-B during World War II congregated at Andersonville on May 3, 1989, 44 years after their liberation, to unveil their memorial.

A NATIONAL MEMORIAL

Today, in the quietness of Andersonville National Cemetery, a sea of marble headstones marks the final resting place of the Union prisoners of war who succumbed to the deprivations of Andersonville. Between 1898 and 1916, states erected monuments to honor their native sons who suffered and perished at the camp. Stone and bronze statues dot the landscape. These silent sentinels stand vigil over the hallowed grounds, keeping an eternal watch over the graves of fallen comrades.

A soldier stands at parade rest atop the New Jersey Monument, the first monument erected. From the Illinois Monument, Columbia extends her hand and directs the attention of "Youth" and "Maiden" to the vast array of headstones and the lessons that they tell. A woman, perhaps a wife or mother, weeps atop the Iowa Monument. Formed in bronze on the New York Monument, an angel descends with victory wreaths to the prisoners below. Other monuments also stand as a reminder of the dedication and patriotism of the prisoners of war interred here—a reminder that their sacrifices will never be forgotten; a testimony to the willingness to endure and even die for one's country.

Encircling the cemetery is this 19th-century brick wall, itself a reminder of a distant time.

A young soldier, his musket turned down, stands solemnly atop the granite base of the Minnesota Monument. The contract for the monument stipulated that Minnesota granite be used, but due to a large amount of snow on the ground at the quarry, Vermont granite was used instead.

Three striking figures, faces grim and gaunt, stand solemnly at the entrance to the national cemetery. Sculptor William Thompson's bronze and marble design was selected over other entries to be the state of Georgia's memorial to all American prisoners of war. Commissioned by Governor Jimmy Carter, the monument was unveiled in 1976.

The contemplative look of a Civil War veteran mingles with light and shadows as dawn's light bathes the Illinois Monument.

The Illinois Monument reminds us that Andersonville should always be remembered. Columbia extends her arm and points to the weathered headstones below, while "Youth" and "Maiden" stand attentively before her, absorbing the lessons of history.

Overleaf: Bronze and brick at the Prisoner of War Commemorative Courtyard echo the pain of captivity.

23

More soldiers from New York were confined at Andersonville than from any other state. Two bronze statues on the New York Monument pay honor to those soldiers. One depicts an angel descending into the prison with olive branches in hand as a symbol of peace. The other shows two soldiers, with both hope and despair reflected on their faces. As a prisoner of war, mental and emotional attitude are as important as one's physical condition.

Bordered by massive magnolias, the Pennsylvania Monument rises from a small knoll in the national cemetery. A bronze plaque on the inside wall depicts prisoners reaching into the deadline with cups to obtain the waters of Providence Spring. The prisoner of war atop the structure was to face North originally. Plans were changed for aesthetic reasons. The lad now faces Americus, Georgia, home of Miller and Clark, the company that constructed the monument.

North and South play a role in many monuments at Andersonville. Granite used in the New York Monument came from North Carolina, while the bronze sculptures were produced by Roman Bronze Works of Brooklyn. The female figure symbolizes the state of New York and holds wreaths to decorate the graves.

Bathed in shadows, this statuary grieves eternally for the sons of Iowa. The Iowa Monument is one of four adorned with a female figure.

Carved from Wisconsin granite and adorned with Corinthian columns, the Indiana Monument was dedicated in November 1908. Dr. R. C. Griffitt, president of the state's Andersonville Monument Commission, stated "we indulge the hope that the flag for which these heroes died will shadow the soil that wraps their clay." The Maine Monument stands in the background, facing North—and the home so many left behind, never to see again.

27

Aftermath

An immediate aftereffect of Andersonville was the arrest and trial of the Swiss immigrant Captain Henry Wirz. Most of the Confederate staff had fled Andersonville by the time Union cavalry arrived in May 1865. Union officers were surprised to find Captain Wirz still at the site. They took him into custody and sent him to Washington, D.C., for trial. Since the commander of the prison camp, General Winder, had died two months before the war ended, Wirz became the target and eventual scapegoat for Andersonville.

There are no crosses or poppies in the national cemetery, but casket-shaped shadows stretch over the final resting-place of Union dead at Andersonville. One-fifth of all Union prisoners who died during the Civil War died at Andersonville. Northern camps were arguably just as bad. Elmira Prison in New York saw over 24 percent of its inhabitants die, the second-worst record of all the Civil War prison camps.

Resting on the prison ground where nearly a thousand Buckeyes lost their lives, the Ohio obelisk rises starkly into the Georgia sky. A combination of Georgia and Ohio granite was used to construct the 48-foot-high monument.

By the time of the military trial which began the last week in August 1865, northern media had reported on the lack of provisions and the high death rate at Andersonville. Photographs showed the living skeletons of Union prisoners of war. There was a public outcry for Wirz to be executed, and the military commissioners seemed willing to appease.

The defense was constantly thwarted, and trial proceedings included much false testimony.

Eyewitnesses recounted how Wirz had personally beaten, shot, and killed prisoners during the most miserable of months, August. No one seemed to heed the fact that Wirz was absent from duty that month due to sickness.

Captain Wirz maintained his innocence throughout the trial. The defense lawyers claimed that their client had only followed orders and did the best he could under the circumstances in which he was placed.

Soldiers and spectators gathered outside the Old Capitol Prison, Washington, D.C., for the execution of Captain Henry Wirz. He was called the demon of Andersonville by some, and considered a hero and martyr to the Confederate cause by others. On May 12, 1909, the United Daughters of the Confederacy dedicated a monument to Wirz in the town of Andersonville. The act was condemned by members of the Grand Army of the Republic during their annual national convention. The debate over Wirz and his innocence or guilt continues to the present day.

COURTESY OF MASSACHUSETTS COMMANDERY MILITARY ORDER OF THE LOYAL LEGION AND THE U.S. ARMY MILITARY HISTORY INSTITUTE

Their arguments were to no avail. Wirz was found guilty of injuring the health and destroying the lives of federal prisoners at Andersonville and "murder, in violation of the laws and customs of war." On November 10, 1865, the sentence was carried out. As soldiers surrounded the gallows, men watched from treetops outside the prison grounds. Some chanted, "Wirz, remember Andersonville." People still have not forgotten.

The true number of victims of Andersonville and other Civil War prison camps will never be known. Surely, many succumbed to health prob-

lems after the war. One tragic post-war incident took the lives of over 1,200 former prisoners of war. Many survivors of Andersonville and Cahaba Prison in Alabama boarded a steamer in Vicksburg, Mississippi, joyful that they were finally heading home. The steamer *Sultana*, extremely overcrowded, headed north against the high waters and rapid currents of the Mississippi River. Just north of Memphis, Tennessee, a boiler exploded, sending passengers into the floodwaters. The *Sultana* incident became the greatest maritime disaster in American history.

Today, the Andersonville Welcome Center greets visitors alongside the same railroad bed that brought Union prisoners into the town during the last 14 months of the Civil War. The original railroad depot has long since been replaced, but trains still rumble by the quiet town, a reminder of days gone by. A few antique and gift shops, along with a Civil War museum, line the main street, all within view of the white obelisk that honors Henry Wirz and dominates the town's landscape.

PRIVATE OWNERSHIP AGAIN

At Andersonville, soon after the end of the Civil War, the prison site reverted back to private ownership. The stockade walls slowly deteriorated. Parts of the wall were taken as souvenirs during reunions of Union veterans and ended up as walking canes, plaques, and other items. Cotton plants soon covered the ground once inhabited by thousands of Union soldiers.

In 1891 the Grand Army of the Republic (GAR), a Union veterans organization, purchased most of the prison site and surrounding earthworks for $1,550. Improvements were made to the site by the Georgia Division, but it soon became apparent that additional funds were needed to develop the area. In 1896, the prison site was acquired by the auxiliary of the GAR, the Womans Relief Corps (WRC). The WRC also purchased the remaining tract of the prison from local landowners. The Womans Relief Corps planted pecan trees along roads at the prison. The nuts, they surmised, could be sold and the money used for maintenance of the area. Like the GAR, maintenance of the site proved to be beyond their means—and in 1910, they sold the land to the United States government for one dollar.

Perhaps no other person worked as hard to preserve Andersonville Prison as Womans Relief Corps President Lizabeth Turner. A monument in honor of Turner was erected at the prison site ten years after her death.

The Prison Park and National Cemetery were administered by the War Department, and later the Department of the Army, until 1970. In that year, the Andersonville National Historic Site was established to "provide an understanding of the overall prisoner of war story of the Civil War, to interpret the role of prisoner of war camps in history, to commemorate the sacrifices of Americans who lost their lives in such camps, and to preserve the monuments located therein."

Although other prison camps during the Civil War, North and South, suffered from mismanagement and high death rates, Andersonville came to symbolize man's inhumanity to man. Twenty-nine percent of its prisoners of war died. Elmira Prison (New York), referred to by many as

States large and small paid a price at Andersonville. The state seal of Rhode Island hangs over the names of its men who lost their lives at the prison camp.

The granite of the Michigan Monument absorbs the pale light of evening. On these same prison grounds over 1,400 Michigan soldiers watched similar nights descend and envelop their world. The artistically carved sculpture seems to cast her thoughts back to those evenings and the lonely souls who called Andersonville home.

The National Park Service has recreated portions of the 1864 prison camp, complete with stockade, deadline, and guard towers. Volunteers and park staff keep shebangs built to interpret the living conditions of the prisoners, and living history programs illustrate the hardships of both prisoners and guards. One can envision the skeletal forms of Union prisoners milling about the stockade, giving the scene a surreal affect.

the "Andersonville of the North," saw almost twenty-five percent of its Confederate prisoners of war perish. The stigma of Camp Sumter continued beyond the American Civil War. During World War II, Camp O'Donnell in the Philippines held survivors of the Bataan Death March and became known as the "Andersonville of the Pacific." In 1998, a national museum was built to interpret the story of the American prisoner of war and commemorate the sacrifices of the individuals held in such camps. The place: Andersonville.

SUGGESTED READING

DAVIS, WILLIAM C. "JACK." *Civil War Parks: The Story Behind the Scenery*. Las Vegas, Nevada: KC Publications, 1984.

DOYLE, ROBERT C. *Voices From Captivity: Interpreting the American POW Narrative*. Lawrence: University Press of Kansas, 1994.

FUTCH, OVID L. *History of Andersonville Prison*. Gainesville: University of Florida Press, 1968.

MARVEL, WILLIAM. *Andersonville: The Last Depot*. Chapel Hill: The University of North Carolina Press, 1994.

POTTER, JERRY O. *The Sultana Tragedy*. Gretna, Louisiana: Pelican Publishing Company, 1992.

RANSOM, JOHN. *John Ransom's Diary*. New York: Paul S. Eriksson, 1963.

SEGARS, J. H. *Andersonville: The Southern Perspective*. Atlanta, Georgia: Southern Heritage Press, 1995.

National Prisoner of War Museum

Freedom does not come free. No one can attest to this better than the men and women who have served in the military. No one knows better what it is like to have that freedom suddenly snatched away than those individuals who, in the process of serving their country, have found themselves prisoners of war. It is an experience neither asked for nor desired. Most Americans who have been prisoners of war are ordinary people who have been placed in extraordinary circumstances by no planning of their own. Americans have been held captive as prisoners of war during many wars and in many places. Still, there is a common bond that is shared by all. Their story is an inspiring chapter of our history as a nation.

The National Prisoner of War Museum is dedicated to all Americans who have been prisoners of war. From the darkness outside, the view through iron gates focuses one's gaze to the interior lights and the illumination of the red, white, and blue of Old Glory. Many have been held captive and have died for love of flag and country.

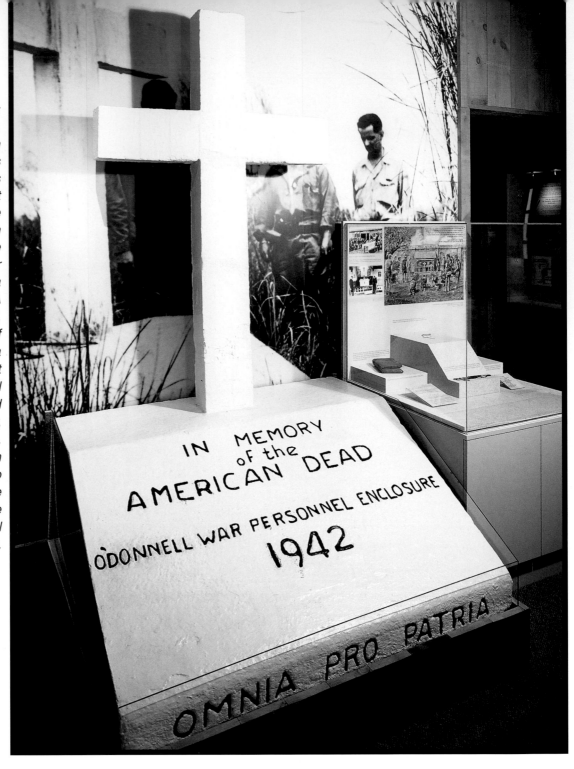

"Omnia Pro Patria": All For the Fatherland. At the end of the Bataan Death March, thousands of American prisoners of war were interned at Camp O'Donnell in the Philippines. As the death rate rose, the Japanese provided cement for the Americans to build a shrine to their dead. A committee was formed, and the consensus of the group was to build a cross. The "Sack of Cement Cross" or "O'Donnell Cross" was built and placed in the nearby cemetery, where it stood for 50 years. In 1992 the eight-foot-high cross was presented to the National Park Service and is the largest single artifact in the National Prisoner of War Museum.

On April 9, 1942, on a peninsula in the Philippines, 10,000 American soldiers became prisoners of war of the Japanese. Bataan had fallen. Exactly 56 years later, over 4,000 former prisoners of war, including survivors of Bataan, and guests gathered at Andersonville National Historic Site for the grand opening of the National Prisoner of War Museum. For many, it was a time to reminisce, to be thankful they had made it through their ordeal, and to remember those who did not return.

THE BUILDING

The national memorial to American prisoners of war, the museum is an imposing red brick structure with few windows. Three granite "guard towers" rise above the roofline and visually dominate the building. The walkway to the museum is flanked by massive iron gates. The architectural elements create a feeling of confinement and provide the beginning of an emotional journey into the museum and the prisoner of war story.

Various methods of confinement have been used to intern prisoners of war throughout United States history. During the Vietnam War, Americans in and around Hanoi were held in prisons they dubbed with nicknames such as Alcatraz, Heartbreak Hotel, and the Hanoi Hilton. Their rooms were no more than small concrete cells, and physical torture was a routine occurrence. In the countryside, other methods of confinement were used. Some prisoners of war were interned in "tiger cages," small bamboo boxes not large enough to stand in. This reproduction cage was built by the U.S. military for the museum.

I learned the human body can suffer nearly everything and still survive

World War II POW

Two wars during the 19th century produced two prison camps with frightening reputations—Dartmoor and Andersonville. During the War of 1812, the stone walls of Dartmoor Prison held thousands of American prisoners and provided little protection from the inclement weather along the English coast. Half a century later, Americans faced similar challenges within the confines of the wooden stockade at Andersonville. Both prisons held their share of misery. The words of Charles Andrews, a Dartmoor prisoner, could have described either camp when he wrote "death itself, with hopes of an hereafter, seemed less terrible than this gloomy prison."

The entry to "Living Conditions" is marked by a panel exemplifying the will of the human spirit to survive. The prisoner of war often suffers at the hands of his or her captors. Physical and mental torture, lack of proper food and water, lack of shelter and clothing, and unsanitary facilities are often the rule rather than the exception in the prisoner of war experience. At various times in American prisoner of war history, prisoners have subsisted on balls of rice, black bread with sawdust, or mealy cornmeal.

Once inside, a large skylight allows light and warmth into the room—a contrast to the cold, dark story of internment which the museum tells. Images high on the lobby walls illustrate the common bond of American prisoners of war. Among the figures, a Civil War soldier assists a World War I prisoner of war. Tri-corner hats, round metal helmets, sailors, and infantry mingle together and lean on each other for support. The prisoner of war story spans the ages.

(text continues on page 45)

At the moment of capture, you are in the hands of your enemy. You are stripped of your weapons, your valuables, your humanity. You no longer control your destiny. You are a prisoner of war.

For those who survive capture, next comes the journey to camp. The journey is often perilous and long. Forced marches are not uncommon. Many have heard or read of the Bataan Death March from World War II, but few are aware that many Americans also died during long marches in Europe near the end of the war. Forced marches during the Korean War, shown in this exhibit photo, often occurred during winter when temperatures were well below freezing.

The realization comes that everything you are left with becomes invaluable once captured. Richard Throckmorton, a World War II prisoner in Germany, recalled: "During that march I did not take my shoes off because the blood was coming through my shoes from the blisters that had broken and I knew that if I took them off I wouldn't be able to get them back on and be able to walk."

Civilians have often been interned as a result of the misfortunes of war. Fern Harrington Miles was in her thirties when captured by the Japanese and held at Bilibid prison camp in the Philippines. The soles of her wooden clogs are tire treads.

John McCambridge was serving in the Pacific aboard the U.S.S. Canopus when war was declared. With the fall of the Philippines, he and the crew soon became prisoners of war. Although many personal possessions were confiscated, he was able to retain his government-issued metal mess kit. The mess kit divulges several things about its owner, including his pride in the Navy and a record of his ship's involvement in the Pacific. Common items such as mess kits and canteens frequently become prisoner of war art as captives use resources at hand to bide their time and express their feelings.

The Ballad of Tom Gordy

In '41 the Japanese
  took our troops on Guam,
Alive or dead - we didn't know
  One was my Uncle Tom

He was the Navy boxing champ,
  my hero with his crown.
Now with him gone, his family moved
  down to our Georgia town.

My grandma and my aunts felt Tom
  was not his wife's but theirs.
She could feel the coolness but
  stayed on to join their prayers.

What bound them all together was
  the hope and faith and dread.
When two years passed, the dispatch came:
  my Uncle Tom was dead.

His wife and kids moved back out West
  to start their lives again,
And after Tom was gone three years
  she wed a family friend.

The end of war brought startling news:
  Tom Gordy was alive.
Four years he had been digging coal
  deep in a mountainside.

The women took the feeble Tom
  and smothered him with care.
He never would tell anyone
  what happened over there.

Tom Gordy soon regained some strength
  and craved a normal life,
But mother and sisters told him lies
  about his absent wife.

Betraying him. Tom wanted her,
  but couldn't figure how
To bring her back or overcome
  her second marriage vow.

He got four years' back pay and made
  Commander, U.S.N.
It didn't take him long to find
  a woman's love again.

Tom closed the past except when his
  three children came to stay;
When I would mention his first wife
  he'd always turn away.

Once my submarine tied up
  where she lived with her kin.
I went to visit them, afraid
  they wouldn't let me in.

But all the folks they knew were called
  when I first gave my name;
All night we danced and sang because
  at least Tom's nephew came.

Jimmy Carter

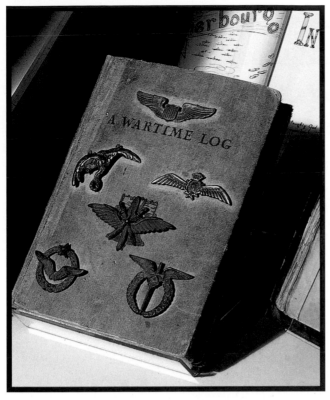

Insignia adorn the cover of this wartime log of an American prisoner held in Germany during World War II. Throughout American history, many prisoners of war have recorded their experiences in diaries and journals. These have provided historians and others with a record of camp conditions, treatment of prisoners, and insight into the psyche of the prisoner of war. Necessity is the mother of invention, and prisoners have substituted bandages and cloth for paper and have even written with their own blood.

One of the greatest desires of a prisoner of war is to regain one's freedom. Escape is often thought of and planned but not always an option. Usually the captive is in a strange land and differs physically from the native people. Unfamiliar surroundings and the threat presented by both armed guards and civilians can present deadly situations. Numerous methods of escape have been employed by prisoners of war, but a mystique seems to persist regarding tunneling. During the Civil War, Union prisoners escaped from Libby Prison in Richmond, Virginia, and numerous tunnels were dug by prisoners at Andersonville. During World War II, American and Allied POWs at Stalag Luft III dug tunnels which led to the "Great Escape." Eighty escaped from the tunnel named Harry, although there were no Americans among them. Only three reached safety. The Code of Conduct, in use today by the military, directs combatants to make every effort to escape.

DEAR EDITH. I WAS VERY GLAD LAST MONTH TO FIND I WAS NOT WHOLLY FORGOTTEN. I'M VERY SORRY I HAVE NOT WRITTEN SOONER BUT I WAS SO SURE I HAD BEEN BUT A MEMORY TO YOU. PLEASE NOTIFY THE FOLKS I AM QUITE WELL. HOPING TO SEE

Captivity is a daily ordeal and plays with the mind as well as the body. A positive attitude is essential to survival, and news from home can be one of the greatest boosts to morale.

Nowhere in the Prisoner of War Museum is the resourcefulness and ingenuity of American prisoners of war more evident than in the theme room "Morale and Relationships." Here rest the O'Donnell Cross, jewelry made by Andersonville prisoners, and one of the most unique artifacts in the museum, an intricate bone ship. During the War of 1812, many French and American prisoners of war were held by Great Britain. A group of prisoners saved beef, mutton, and pork bones from their rations and gradually collected enough to construct this elaborate model.

The award-winning production "Those Who Wait" is one of the most poignant and emotional presentations in the National Prisoner of War Museum. Some families of POWs in Vietnam waited over seven years for their loved one to return. Some have never come home. Over 10,000 soldiers remain missing in action from Korea and Vietnam.

At the entry to the museum exhibits, a panel sums up the mission of the museum: "The National Prisoner of War Museum is dedicated to the men and women of this country who suffered captivity so that others could remain free. Their story is one of sacrifice and courage; their legacy, the gift of liberty."

THE EXPERIENCE

The story of sacrifice and courage, as well as the endurance of the human spirit, is reflected throughout the museum. Utilizing a thematic approach, each room touches upon a common element of the prisoner of war experience—Capture, Journey to Camp, Living Conditions, Communication, Morale and Relationships, and finally, Freedom. An additional exhibit area, Those Who Wait, presents the emotional trials experienced by spouses, children, and other family members of prisoners of war.

As a whole, the museum experience is a microcosm of the prisoner of war experience. As the voices and faces tell their story, you are drawn into their world. You see their determination and feel their hope. You begin to understand the meaning of courage, sacrifice, patriotism, and freedom. You realize that freedom does not come free.

This silk cloth belonged to Harry Kaczorowski of the 34th Infantry Division. Ground troops attached the cloths to their backpacks so aviators could distinguish them from enemy soldiers. Kaczorowski was captured in North Africa in 1943 and was interned in prison camps in Italy, Germany, and Poland. A friend painted the scenes on the cloth during their confinement.

How does it feel to regain freedom? Words are insufficient, but the answer can be seen and felt in the tears of a spouse, the hugs of a child, and the gratitude of a nation.

A mixture of light and shadows combine with artistic elements to lend a reflective beauty to artist Donna Dobberfuhl's creation. Former prisoners of war took an active role in the National Prisoner of War Museum from its inception, and the American Ex-Prisoners of War organization funded construction of the Prisoner of War Commemorative Courtyard.

ANDERSONVILLE
NATIONAL HISTORIC SITE

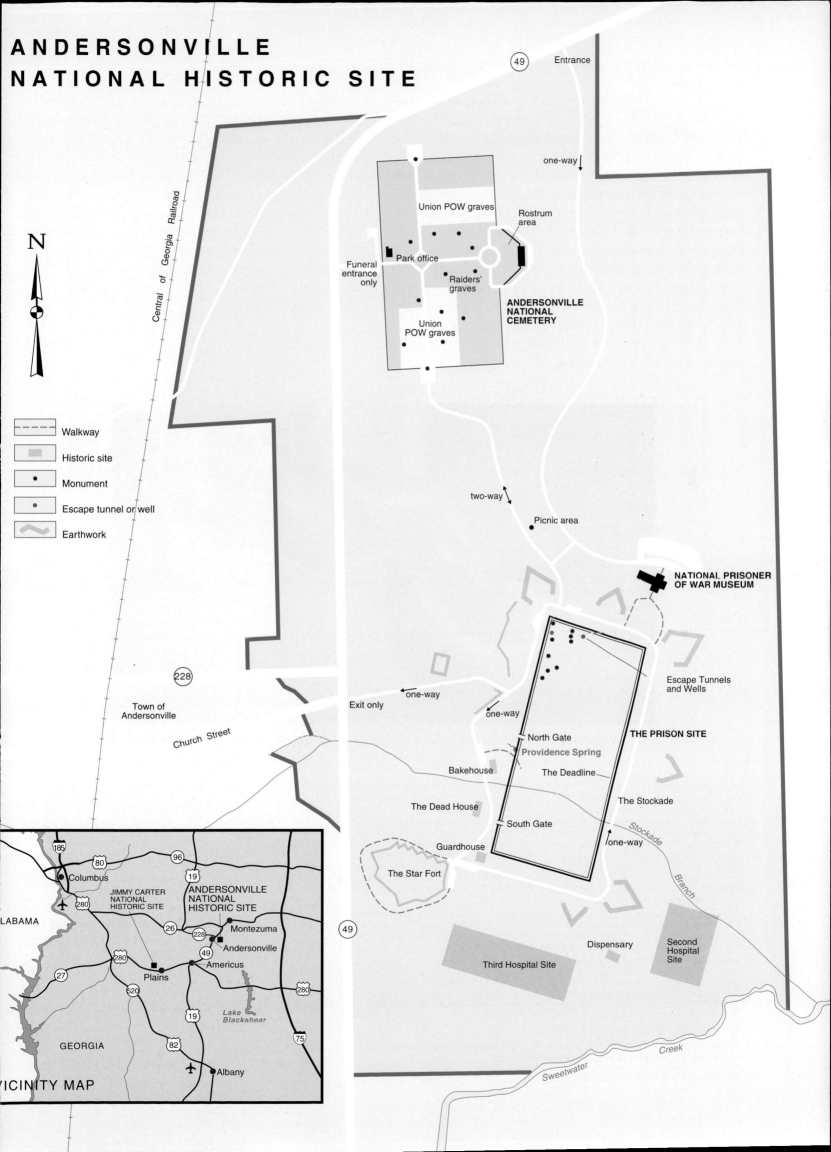

N

Central of Georgia Railroad

(49)   Entrance

one-way ↓

Union POW graves

Rostrum area

Funeral entrance only

Park office

Raiders' graves

Union POW graves

ANDERSONVILLE NATIONAL CEMETERY

--- Walkway

Historic site

• Monument

⊙ Escape tunnel or well

Earthwork

two-way ↕

Picnic area

(228)

NATIONAL PRISONER OF WAR MUSEUM

Escape Tunnels and Wells

one-way →

Exit only

one-way ↙

THE PRISON SITE

Town of Andersonville

Church Street

North Gate

Providence Spring

The Deadline

Bakehouse

The Dead House

The Stockade

South Gate

Guardhouse

one-way ↑

Stockade

Branch

The Star Fort

one-way ↑

(49)

Dispensary

Second Hospital Site

Third Hospital Site

Sweetwater   Creek

VICINITY MAP

(185)

(80)   (96)

Columbus

(19)

JIMMY CARTER NATIONAL HISTORIC SITE

ANDERSONVILLE NATIONAL HISTORIC SITE

ALABAMA

(280)

(26)   (228)   Montezuma

(49)   Andersonville

(27)   (280)   Americus

Plains

(520)

(280)

(19)

Lake Blackshear

(75)

GEORGIA

(82)

Albany

The Lesson

One step out the rear door of the lobby, visitors have a place to catch their breath. The Prisoner of War Commemorative Courtyard is a place to reflect and to contemplate. A small stream flows gently through a granite courtyard and encircles three walls of sculpted brick—men, women, and barbed wire molded from the clay. A bronze statue of a prisoner of war hunches over the water, his eyes gazing toward the heavens, water dripping from his outstretched hands into the stream below. The eyes are melancholy, yet hopeful. They seem to echo the words penned by an Andersonville prisoner of war many years before—"If it weren't for hope the heart would break. And I am hopeful yet."

Many years have passed since the thud of axes on pine signaled the beginning of a prisoner of war camp at Andersonville. Today, the wind gently blows through the trees and across the serene landscape. The horrors of the Civil War have faded but have not been forgotten. Amid the tranquillity is the constant reminder that throughout our country's history, many have experienced hardships, torture, and even death as prisoners of war. Each one has known the true meaning of freedom, for they have had theirs taken away.

The hands have changed, but the gift of freedom has been passed down through generations.

Inside back cover: Prisoners of war have faced the darkness of man's inhumanity to man and have shown us the best of the human spirit.

Back cover: Captured but not defeated, mental fortitude and faith become two of the prisoner of war's greatest allies.

Created, Designed, and Published in the U.S.A.
Ink formulated by Daihan Ink Co., Ltd.
Color separations & printing by Doosan Corporation, Seoul, Korea
Paper produced exclusively by Hankuk Paper Mfg. Co., Ltd.